The Dail

1, 2, & 3 John

Kristi Burchfiel

ISBN-13: **978-1502397713**
ISBN-10: **1502397714**

Cover design by Jonna Feavel
Images used with permission
Swirl ©Andrea Haase|Dreamstime.com
ID 10305230 © Leigh Prather | Dreamstime.com
ID 9806552 © Otnaydur | Dreamstime.com

Unless otherwise identified, all scripture quotations in this publication are taken from *The Holy Bible, New International Version*®, NIV, Copyright © 1973, 1978, 1984, 2011 by Biblica, Inc.

Introduction

What is The Daily Devotional Series?

The Daily Devotional Series was born from my own personal devotions. As part of my daily time with God, I wanted to be able to read and study a whole book of the Bible at a time. However, I also wanted to be able to focus on one specific thought or idea that I could hold on to for the whole day.

This particular book is a little different from my other books in the series. While I still just focus on one, or maybe two verses, each day, I go through each and every verse in these three books. Since 1, 2, and 3 John are shorter books, I wanted to study each verse more in depth, while still staying focused on just one truth for that day.

These devotions are not designed to be an in-depth study of a particular verse, chapter, or book. They are intentionally designed to be brief. Because of this, readers won't get bogged down in lots of theology. Instead, I encourage the reader to take the time to really focus on application in his or her personal life. The Bible is living and active and applicable in our daily lives.

How do I use The Daily Devotional Series?

If you have the time, I encourage you to take the time to read through the entire chapter for each day so you can get the full story and background information. However, realize that is not necessary to be able to follow and learn from the devotionals. Each devotional focuses on one verse, the truth in that verse, and a response to pray back to God.

May you be blessed as you study God's word and apply it to your life daily.

About 1, 2, & 3 John

I love to receive notes of encouragement; as do most people I know. There's something special about hearing from a person who recognizes the work you've been doing and wants to say "great job!" John takes that approach in these three letters. He wants to encourage the believers and recognize the wonderful things they have been part of

All three letters were written within a relatively short period of time, probably between the late 80s and early 90s AD. First John was addressed to all Christians. Second John is addressed to a church, although it doesn't specify a region or area where the church was located. Finally, 3 John is addressed to a person, Gaius, who was probably a preacher or leader over a region of churches. All three books reference the love of God over and over, and that seems to be a recurrent theme for John. John understood the power of the love of God and he sought to have that love permeate every area of his life. Love is so often the focus of every area of his writings, even to the point where he refers to himself as "the disciple whom Jesus loved" all throughout the Gospel of John.

However, John also uses these books to give warnings as well. Several false teachings about Jesus have been circulating and false teachers were traveling around just like the genuine believers and churches were sometimes having a hard time differentiating between the truth and the lies. John addresses this in each book. He wants the believers to understand how to tell the difference and not be swayed in their beliefs because they know what is true.

It's an interesting balance between being able to follow and display the love of God and stay on guard against the lies and false teachings. John handles these two issues beautifully and the Holy Spirit uses him to pen some of the most wonderful words of assurance, love, and hope. We can be confident in all areas of our faith, and John reminds us of that as we glean God's amazing truths through these three wonderful letters.

1 John

Day 1

1 John 1:1—That which was from the beginning, which we have heard, which we have seen with our eyes, which we have looked at and our hands have touched—this we proclaim concerning the Word of life.

TRUTH:
John, the author, had personally experienced Jesus. He walked with Him and talked with Him, now He is sharing what he knows to be true based on his personal experience. When we ask Christ in our lives, we also have personal experience with Jesus. Our testimony of what we have personally experienced in Christ is powerful. People can call us liars, but they cannot disprove what we say. Do we share with others what we have personally experienced concerning our relationship with Jesus Christ?

RESPONSE:
Father, You touch and impact my life every day. You are faithful beyond measure, and I trust in You in all things. I will not be afraid or timid to share what You have done for me. Your personal impact on my life has made all the difference, and I will share with courage and boldness.

Day 2

1 John 1:2—The life appeared; we have seen it and testify to it, and we proclaim to you the eternal life, which was with the Father and has appeared to us.

TRUTH:
Eternal life appears to them. How is that possible? In John 17:3, he defines eternal life as knowing God and Jesus Christ who was sent by God. How can we testify about eternal life? We've experienced Jesus Christ. When we accept Jesus Christ as the Son of God, we invite Him into our life and we experience His life, eternal life. Have we experienced His eternal life? Do we proclaim that life to others?

RESPONSE:
Father, You are eternal life and You freely give that life through Jesus Christ Your Son. I have seen it; I have experienced it. I will proclaim it to everyone.

Day 3

1 John 1:3—We proclaim to you what we have seen and heard, so that you also may have fellowship with us. And our fellowship is with the Father and with his Son, Jesus Christ.

TRUTH:
How do we have fellowship with other believers? Fellowship is not about food or games; fellowship is about sharing what Jesus Christ has done in our life. As we share what we've seen and heard Jesus do, we experience true fellowship, not just with other believers, but also with God himself. When was the last time we shared what we've seen and heard Jesus do in our life? When was the last time we truly experienced fellowship?

RESPONSE:
Father, You are amazing and the things You have done in my life are equally amazing. I will share those with others so that You may be glorified and that I may experience true fellowship with You and with other believers.

Day 4

1 John 1:4—We write this to make our joy complete.

TRUTH:
How do we have and experience complete joy? We experience complete joy when we share with others our experience with Jesus Christ. He is the source of all joy and as we share together with other believers, we experience, not just fellowship, but full and complete joy. Are we experiencing joy in our daily life? If not, then we must not be experiencing true fellowship with other believers and sharing about Christ in our lives? Find someone to share with and watch your joy be made complete.

RESPONSE:
Father, You are joy and You bestow Your joy on Your children. As I focus on You, I see that joy more completely and experience it more fully. Help me to identify opportunities today to share so that I may experience Your complete joy.

Day 5

1 John 1:5—This is the message we have heard from him and declare to you: God is light; in him there is no darkness at all.

TRUTH:
God is light. That is the message that we declare to each other. There is a light in this world that seems so dark and black. We have a means to get out of the darkness that we find around us and go into the light. Are we declaring that God is the light to the world that is lost in darkness?

RESPONSE:
Father, You are light. You are the pure light which has come into the world to banish the darkness. I will declare to everyone that there is hope. You are the hope, for in You there is no darkness at all.

Day 6

1 John 1:6—If we claim to have fellowship with him and yet walk in the darkness, we lie and do not live out the truth.

TRUTH:
Does our walk match our talk? If we show up to church on Sunday and state that we are following Christ, but then live in disobedience the rest of the week, we are lying. We're lying to ourselves, to others, and to God. We can't live out the truth if we are busy lying. Do our actions match our words?

RESPONSE:
Father, You are truth and I will live out the truth. Help me identify areas in my life where my actions are not in line with my words and desire to follow You. I surrender those areas to You. I desire to live and walk in the light.

Day 7

1 John 1:7—But if we walk in the light, as he is in the light, we have fellowship with one another, and the blood of Jesus his Son, purifies us from all sin.

TRUTH:
God is light, and we are to walk each day in the light. That's where He is, so that's where we are to be. When we are in the light, walking and being obedient to God, then we experience two things: fellowship and purification. Through Christ, we experience true fellowship with each other and we are purified from our sins. Do we feel alone or are we consumed by our sins? God is the answer and we are to walk with Him in the light of truth.

RESPONSE:
Father, the darkness is lies and deception. However, the light is truth, fellowship, and freedom from sin. I will join You in the light today. The blood of Jesus purifies me and makes me clean from sin so that I may enjoy fellowship with You and with others who follow You.

Day 8

1 John 1:8—If we claim to be without sin, we deceive ourselves and the truth is not in us.

TRUTH:
"I'm not so bad. There are plenty of people around who do worse things than I do." I've said this before, have you? It's a lie, pure and simple. We are all sinners in need of God's forgiveness and grace. If we tell ourselves anything else, we're lying to ourselves. We must be honest with ourselves about who we are and what we've done. Then, we must be honest with God. We may not be perfect, but praise God, we can be forgiven!

RESPONSE:
Father, I am not perfect and any attempt to tell myself that I am perfect is doomed to failure. You are truth and You are forgiveness. I will not deceive myself into thinking that I am better than I am. I am not. Thank You for Your grace for me, a sinner.

Day 9

1 John 1:9—If we confess our sins, he is faithful and just and will forgive us our sins and purify us from all unrighteousness.

TRUTH:
Our responsibility is to confess, not ask for forgiveness. God promises us that He will forgive us and cleanse us if we will only confess. What does it mean to confess? When we confess, we see our sins as God sees them. We understand that God is holy and we recognize the gravity of our failings in comparison to Him. As we come to Him desiring to turn away from these sins, He hears us, forgives us, and purifies us.

RESPONSE:
Father, Your word is truth. You are holy and righteous and I am not. I have fallen short in so many ways. I see my failings for what they are and I know without Your promise of forgiveness and cleansing, I will never be clean. Thank You for hearing me, forgiving me, and purifying me.

Day 10

1 John 1:10—If we claim we have not sinned, we make him out to be a liar and his word is not in us.

TRUTH:
Do we talk like we are perfect? Do we act like we are perfect? Only God is perfect. If we are claiming it, we are lying to ourselves, others, and God. We cannot truly understand God and His sacrifice on our behalf if we think we aren't in need of a sacrifice. God's word points us to our need of a sacrifice. God's word points us to our need for a Savior. Do we acknowledge our need for a Savior, or are we a liar?

RESPONSE:
Father, I am not perfect. I know that, yet sometimes because of pride I try to act like I'm better than I really am. I confess that is wrong. I will depend on You to make it through. Thank You for all You have done for me! I love You!

Day 11

1 John 2:1—My dear children, I write this to you so that you will not sin. But if anybody does sin, we have an advocate with the Father—Jesus Christ the Righteous One.

TRUTH:
Since we've already established that we are all sinners in previous verses, it is such great news to know that we have an advocate. Jesus Christ, the Righteous One, has bridged the gap between our sin and God's holiness. He stands in the middle as an intermediary who loves us and desires to see us restored to God. He acts on our behalf. Have we sought out our advocate? Jesus Christ is always there for us.

RESPONSE:
Father, You have made a way for me, a sinner, to have access to You, the Holy One. Jesus Christ is my advocate and He stands up for me. Thank You for standing up on my behalf!

Day 12

1 John 2:2—He is the atoning sacrifice for our sins, and not only for ours but also for the sins of the whole world.

TRUTH:
Jesus Christ came and died as the sacrifice for our sins. He rose victorious and He lives, allowing us to live in Him. However, this gift is not just for a select few. His sacrifice is available to all who will believe in Him. Are we willing to share with all people or do we only share this message for good news with a select few? His sacrifice was for the whole world; the whole world needs to know.

RESPONSE:
Father, Your gift of eternal life is available to all who will believe You and accept the sacrifice of Jesus Christ. Lord, You are over all and only through Jesus Christ can we be made right with You.

Day 13

1 John 2:3—We know that we have come to know him if we keep his commandments.

TRUTH:
We have a way to check ourselves and make sure that we know God. If we are keeping His commands, then we know Him. If we aren't, we don't. This sounds simplistic, yet it is absolutely true. As we go through the day, if we are acting out the things we have heard and learned from Jesus Christ, then we truly know Him. Our actions must line up with our words, which all must line up with Christ.

RESPONSE:
Father, I will learn more about You every day. As I know You more, I will act like You more. You have done all things for me and You have a response for every area of my life. I will follow through in the same way that You would have me respond.

Day 14

1 John 2:4—Whoever says, "I know him," but does not do what he commands is a liar, and the truth is not in that person.

TRUTH:
Do we know God? More important than how we verbally answer that question, though, is how our life answers that question. Do our actions confirm the truth of our words or do they prove we are a liar? Our words are important and our actions must match the words that we say.

RESPONSE:
Father, my words and actions must go together. I will follow Your commands and will ensure that my actions convey the truth of my words. I love You and desire to follow You in every area of my life.

Day 15

1 John 2:5-6—But if anyone obeys his word, love for God is truly made complete in them. This is how we know we are in him: Whoever claims to live in him must live as Jesus did.

TRUTH:
As we obey God more, we love God more. This is a ratio that is constant. When we love God more, we will obey God more. As we obey God more, we will love God more. We can use this as a measure to know and understand how to live like Jesus did. When we are living each day fully obedient to God, we demonstrate love of God to ourselves and everyone around us. Are we displaying God's love to everyone?

RESPONSE:
Father, if I want to love You more, I must obey You more. As I obey You more, I will see and feel Your love more. Help me to never lose sight of Your love and my need to live each day as Jesus did.

Day 16

1 John 2:7—Dear friends, I am not writing you a new command but an old one, which you have had since the beginning. This old command is the message you have heard.

TRUTH:
They needed to be reminded of what they already knew. God had commanded them to love others, this was not new. However, they needed a reminder and a refresher. God had provided them a new example of love through Jesus Christ, which we'll talk about tomorrow, but the command to love one another was old. Are we doing what we know to do and what we have been told to do, or are we distracted by things that have gotten in the way and turned us aside from what we know?

RESPONSE:
Father, thank You for the reminder to focus on the things I know to do. I appreciate all that You have done, and I will go back to the single-minded focus on Your commands. I will love others as You love.

Day 17

1 John 2:8—Yet I am writing you a new command; its truth is seen in him and in you, because the darkness is passing and the true light is already shining.

TRUTH:
The darkness is passing. Why is the darkness passing away? The true light is already shining. We have seen the true light, and He is the example of the command to love others. Jesus Christ is the light, and He came so that we could all see and experience the true light for ourselves.

RESPONSE:
Father, You are truly amazing and You are the true light that scatters the darkness. The command to love others will be my command, and I will follow through on that with Your help. I will not focus on the darkness because it is passing away.

Day 18

1 John 2:9—Anyone who claims to be in the light but hates a brother or sister is still in the darkness.

TRUTH:
Our relationships with others matter. We cannot claim to be followers of Jesus Christ and then hate the Christians we are around. We can't say we love Christ, but hate going to church. Christ is the light and we must see others in that light if we are truly allowing Christ in our life. How do we treat and respond to others?

RESPONSE:
Father, You are truly the light in the world and in my life. I will use Your light to view all the people around me so I am able to see and treat others the way You would. I love You and thank You for all You have done for me. Thank You for being at the center of all my relationships.

Day 19

1 John 2:10-11—Anyone who loves their brother and sister lives in the light, and there is nothing in them to make them stumble. But anyone who hates a brother or sister is in the darkness and walks around in the darkness. They do not know where they are going, because the darkness has blinded them.

TRUTH:
The way we treat other believers is very telling. We can say all we want, but unless we are allowing our actions to demonstrate love toward other believers, we are not truly walking in the light ourselves. As Christians, we each have Christ in us and Christ will not hate Himself. If we try to hate a fellow believer, we are showing that Christ is not truly Lord of our life in that area because Christ would love Himself. Do we stumble in the darkness of hate or are we walking in the light of love?

RESPONSE:
Father, help me see each and every believer as if I were seeing You, and therefore I will love them as I love You. I will not be distracted by anything else, but will remember Your love for them and seek to walk in the light.

Day 20

1 John 2:12-13—I am writing to you, dear children, because your sins have been forgiven on account of his name. I am writing to you, fathers, because you know him who is from the beginning. I am writing to you, young men, because you have overcome the evil one.

TRUTH:
Our sins have been forgiven, Jesus has been constant from the beginning, and through Jesus we have overcome the evil one. These are the reasons that John lists for why he is writing this letter to the people. We have such great and immeasurable hope! Circumstances can weigh down on us, but we are rewarded that we are forgiven, Christ is victorious, and though Him we will overcome the evil one! Do we believe that? Do we live that out every day?

RESPONSE:
Father, circumstances have a way of creeping into my mind and making me think they are bigger than they are. You are over everything. You are victorious, and I will place my hope in You. I will confidently face the day knowing that You are my reason for hope.

Day 21

1 John 2:14—I write to you, dear children, because you know the Father. I write to you, fathers, because you know him who is from the beginning. I write to you, young men, because you are strong, and the word of God lives in you, and you have overcome the evil one.

TRUTH:
The believers that John wrote to knew God and because they did, they were strong and the Word of God lived in them. Because the Word of God lived in them, they were able to overcome the evil one. How do we overcome the evil one? We overcome through the Word of God. It is the recipe for being able to make it through anything that Satan throws our way. God's Word is eternal. Through God's Word we know God and we become strong. As we share God's Word with each other and allow it to live in and through us, we are able to defeat the evil one.

RESPONSE:
Father, You were from the beginning and Your Word was from the beginning. I will hold to Your Word and allow it to live in and through me in everything that I do. Through Your Word in me I will overcome evil because You overcome evil. Live in and through me today.

Day 22

1 John 2:15—Do not love the world or anything in the world. If anyone loves the world, love for the Father is not in them.

TRUTH:
This is an either/or situation. We either love God or we love the world. Since they stand for exactly the opposite things, we cannot love both of them. When we love something, we are committed to it and will do anything for it. Are we focused on God and on loving God? Anything else is simply going against God.

RESPONSE:
Father, You are my only love. I will love You and through You, You are able to show love to the others in my life. Nothing will come between me and my love for You.

Day 23

1 John 2:16—For everything in the world—the lust of the flesh, the lust of the eyes, and the pride of life—comes not from the Father but from the world.

TRUTH:
God is the Creator. However as we are living in the world, we have perverted the perfection of God's creation. Lust and pride came into the world and tempts us to value God's creation more than we value the Creator Himself. Those temptations come in three categories: the flesh, the eyes, and the pride of life. Are we being drawn away from the Creator by the temptations that come and appeal to us in every one of these areas?

RESPONSE:
Father, I will keep my eye on the Creator, You, and will not focus on the flashy distractions of the world. You are what I desire, not the world.

Day 24

1 John 2:17—The world and its desires pass away, but whoever does the will of God lives forever.

TRUTH:
Are we focusing on something eternal or on something temporary? The temptations we covered yesterday are always there trying to lead us away, yet, these are temporary and are passing away. As we submit ourselves to God, we will be following Him and will live forever with Him. Are we going after what will pass away or what will remains forever?

RESPONSE:
Father, You and Your will is what is eternal. I will seek You and Your desires and will follow after You. I praise You and will not be distracted today by the things that will eventually pass away.

Day 25

1 John 2:18—Dear children, this is the last hour; and as you have heard that the antichrist is coming, even now many antichrists have come. This is how we know it is the last hour.

TRUTH:
In this verse, antichrist refers to being "against" Christ. Just like now, as we continue into the last days, John was faced with several people and ideas that were against Christ. Do we readily identify those things that are against Christ or do we get deceived? We must follow God and keep our eyes on Him and not be distracted and turned away by all the things out there that are against Christ.

RESPONSE:
Father, there are so many "antichrists" out in our world today pulling me and trying to entice me to stop looking at You. I will focus on You today and remember to follow only You.

Day 26

1 John 2:19—They went out from us, but they did not really belong to us. For it they had belonged to us, they would have remained with us; but their going showed that none of them belonged to us.

TRUTH:
Not everyone who goes to church belongs to Christ. In fact, many people who enter church and seem to say the right things while they are there, end up leaving and don't really follow through or act on anything they heard or said at church. We must be careful not to follow their example. If we truly belong to God, we will seek to remain in God's will and in His presence all the time, not just when it's convenient or when others are watching.

RESPONSE:
Father, You are all I want and I desire to stay where You are. I will not leave and I will not follow those people who are only at church for show. I belong to You.

Day 27

1 John 2:20-21—But you have an anointing from the Holy One, and all of you know the truth. I do not write to you because you do not know the truth, but because you do know it and because no lie comes from the truth.

TRUTH:
As we live in the truth of Jesus Christ and allow Him to lead and direct us, we experience an anointing from the Holy Spirit. The Holy Spirit enables us to live out the truth that is in our lives. Jesus Christ is the truth and the Holy Spirit gives us the power and ability to walk in the truth each day. Are we living out the walk of Jesus Christ through the power of the Holy Spirit?

RESPONSE:
Father, I praise You and know that You are the truth in life. I will live out Your power and truth through Your Holy Spirit today.

Day 28

1 John 2:22-23—Who is the liar? It is whoever denies that Jesus is the Christ. Such a person is the antichrist—denying the Father and the Son. No one who denies the Son has the Father; whoever acknowledges the Son has the Father also.

TRUTH:
What is our relationship with Jesus Christ? Ultimately, everything comes down to that question. If we deny that Jesus is the Christ, the Son of God, then we are liars and are against God. We cannot claim to have God or be a part of God and yet deny the place and position of Jesus. Only through our relationship with Jesus Christ do we have a real relationship with God. We cannot have it any other way.

RESPONSE:
Father, I acknowledge and accept Your position, and I believe and receive Jesus Christ as the Lord of all, including my entire life. I pray that others will see that through my life as I acknowledge You.

Day 29

1 John 2:24-25—As for you, see that what you have heard from the beginning remains in you. If it does, you also will remain in the Son and in the Father. And this is what he promised us—eternal life.

TRUTH:
We are to remain steadfast in what God has taught us. We are to consistently follow through on His direction and His teaching. He has promised that as we do that, He will remain in us and He will provide us eternal life. Are we remaining steadfast in all that He has commanded us?

RESPONSE:
Father, I will remain steadfast in all that You desire for me. I pray You will help me see Your promises every day as You are providing what You promised, eternal life.

Day 30

1 John 2:26—I am writing these things to you about those who are trying to lead you astray.

TRUTH:
Warning! John is delivering a warning to the people that they must be on their guard because there are people who are trying to lead them astray from God. There are plenty of people who are trying to distract us and turn us away from what God has for us. Are we guarding our hearts and our minds so that we are not led astray?

RESPONSE:
Father, thank You for providing a warning so that I know I need to be on guard. I will stand guard over my heart and mind against those who would try to distract me or lead me astray from following You.

Day 31

1 John 2:27—As for you, the anointing you received from him remains in you, and you do not need anyone to teach you. But as his anointing teaches you about all things and as that anointing is real, not counterfeit—just as it has taught you, remain in him.

TRUTH:
John has already mentioned in previous verses that they had received the anointing from the Holy One who is truth. In that day, others were coming to the Christians claiming to have "additional" truth and wanting to teach them. John wants us to know that when we have the Truth, Jesus Christ, we don't need anything else to add to it. Receiving teaching about Jesus and following up on the things of Jesus is to be our truth. We should not seek to add anything else to the message of Jesus.

RESPONSE:
Father, I love You and desire to be with You and seek You and You only. You are the Truth and I don't need anything else except You. Help me guard against relying on anything else except You.

Day 32

1 John 2:28—And now, dear children, continue in him, so that when he appears we may be confident and unashamed before him at his coming.

TRUTH:
Would you want Jesus with you today? We are to continue in Him so we would not be ashamed at His coming. What if He came today? Is there anything you would be doing that you would do differently knowing Jesus would sit beside you? Would you alter your TV shows or your business meetings or your dinner plans? We are to continue through each day as though we are confident and unashamed of Him regardless of what He would find us doing each day.

RESPONSE:
Father, I know You are with me always, but sometimes I forget that and don't act like it. I pray You will keep me focused on You so that no matter what I am doing, I will be confidently continuing in You.

Day 33

1 John 2:29—If you know that he is righteous, you know that everyone who does what is right has been born of him.

TRUTH:
We know that God is righteous. He is perfect in all that He does. If we are following Him, we will be acting the same way that He acts. Are others able to tell that we are a follower of Christ based on how we act each day? Do our responses line up with God's word?

RESPONSE:
Father, if I say I follow You, then all I do should be a match for all that You do. I will seek to learn and know You and allow You to live through me so that my actions will line up with Yours today.

Day 34

1 John 3:1—See what great love the Father has lavished on us, that we should be called children of God! And that is what we are! The reason the world does not know us is that it did not know him.

TRUTH:
We are so privileged to be called the children of God and that is through the great love that God has for us. He made a way for us to come to him that the world does not understand. They don't know or respect us because they don't know or respect God. As we reflect God, they will turn away from us also. Are we living in the lavish love of our Father or are we choosing the love of the world? We cannot have both.

RESPONSE:
Father, Your love is all I want. You have called me Your child and I can't believe or explain why other than the fact that You love me. I will seek after and follow You and Your love for me, not the world's love.

Day 35

1 John 3:2—Dear friends, now we are children of God, and what we will be has not been made known. But we know that when Christ appears, we shall be like him for we shall see him as he is.

TRUTH:
Once we have asked Jesus into our hearts, we are in the process of being made like Jesus. One day, we will be completely changed, but in the meantime, we are being molded and made more like Him every day. We may not know exactly what that looks like, but we know that God knows both the process and the finished product. We can trust Him as we seek to be more like Him every day.

RESPONSE:
Father, You know the end result of my becoming more like You, and You know what steps it will take to help me get there. I will trust You to lead me in the right path that will lead and mold me to be more like You.

Day 36

1 John 3:3—All who have this hope in him purify themselves, just as he is pure.

TRUTH:
As mentioned yesterday, we have the hope of being made like Him. We have that so, so how should we respond? We should be purifying ourselves. Now, since we cannot make ourselves pure, we must come to God and allow Him to work in our life to purify us. We can have full confidence in God's ability to purify us as we are seeking Him.

RESPONSE:
Father, You are pure and in You I place my hope. I will have full confidence that all You have promised, You will do.

Day 37

1 John 3:4-5—Everyone who sins breaks the law; in fact, sin is lawlessness. But you know that he appeared so that he might take away our sins. And in him is no sin.

TRUTH:
Jesus came so that we would be made right with God. Our sin keeps us from being right with Him and is an example of us breaking the law. However, with Jesus, we have our sins taken away from us. He's forgiven them and in Jesus there is no sin. As we surrender our life to Jesus, we have the realization that He wants to live in and through us. That way we know what is right and what is wrong.

RESPONSE:
Father, You are perfect and Your Son Jesus is perfect. Thank You for providing a way for my sins to be forgiven and taken away. You are with me and I will seek You and rely on You to lead me in each decision today.

Day 38

1 John 3:6—No one who lives in him keeps on sinning. No one who continues to sin has either seen him or known him.

TRUTH:
When we come to God and repent of our sin, God forgives us and makes us new. Since we are new, we now have new desires and new thoughts. Sure, those old, sinful thoughts will still surface and try to lead us astray. However, we can hold fast to God, knowing that He lives in us and through Him, we can be victorious over the temptations that come our way today.

RESPONSE:
Father, You have given us a wonderful chance to be part of You. Thank You for giving me victory over my temptations. I desire to live in You today.

Day 39

1 John 3:7—Dear children, do not let anyone lead you astray. The one who does what is right is righteous, just as he is righteous.

TRUTH:
How are we righteous? We are made righteous through Jesus and by following Him. He is righteous and as we do what He would have us do, we will be righteous. We must be careful that we aren't deceived or led astray thinking that we can be made right with God by any other way. Only Jesus is righteous and only through Him will we be made righteous.

RESPONSE:
Father, You are holy and righteous. I will not be distracted or led astray, but will focus on You. No one else can do what You've promised and I will allow Your righteousness to work through me today.

Day 40

1 John 3:8—The one who does what is sinful is of the devil, because the devil has been sinning from the beginning. The reason the Son of God appeared was to destroy the devil's work.

TRUTH:
If the one who does what is right is righteous, like it says in the previous verse, then the one who does what is sinful is of the devil. Satan has been sinning and leading others into sin since the beginning. However, we are not left to fall into Satan's hands. God sent Jesus Christ to come and destroy what Satan had done, however, we must accept His free gift of life. Do we live each day victorious knowing all that Christ has done for us?

RESPONSE:
Father, I don't have to live under the evil schemes of the devil anymore. You came and destroyed his plans for my destruction and by accepting You, I can be righteous as You are righteous. I love You and I'm excited that You have made a way for me as well as for others who will accept You.

Day 41

1 John 3:9—No one who is born of God will continue to sin, because God's seed remains in them; they cannot go on sinning, because they have been born of God.

TRUTH:
What characterizes our life? Do people look at our life and see us seeking after God and Godly things, or do people see us seeking after things of the world? We will never be perfect while we are here on earth, but we can be living a life that is characterized by our trust in God. Have we asked God to be part of our life? Then all we do will be indicative of Him working in and through us.

RESPONSE:
Lord, help me to respond correctly when I have been hurt and betrayed. Take my hurt and heal it so that only Your feelings of forgiveness remain.

Day 42

1 John 3:10—This is how we know who the children of God are and who the children of the devil are: Anyone who does not do what is right is not God's child, nor is anyone who does not love their brother and sister.

TRUTH:
We can share with people through our words whether or not we are followers of Jesus, but it's by our actions that we give meaning and life to our words. Our actions are easily visible and easily identifiable as to whether we are seeking God or not. How will others perceive our actions? Will we be easily identified as a follower of Christ or not?

RESPONSE:
Father, some days it's a struggle to act like You would have me act. Yet I want my actions to be a clear indication of my devotion to You. Keep me focused on You today. Do not let my actions fall away from pointing people to You.

Day 43

1 John 3:11-12—For this is the message you heard from the beginning: We should love one another. Do not be like Cain, who belonged to the evil one and murdered his brother. And why did he murder him? Because his own actions were evil and his brother's were righteous.

TRUTH:
Cain murdering his brother Abel is a perfect example of evil lashing out at righteousness. Abel was pleasing before the Lord and Cain was jealous. Instead of that spurring Cain to repentance and restoration with God, he became bitter and angry and ultimately destroyed his brother simply because Abel was righteous. When we fall short of God's desires for our life, do we get angry at others who are still following God? Or instead, do we turn to God and seek His forgiveness and His restoration?

RESPONSE:
Father, I will not allow sin in my life to drive a wedge between me and others who are following You. I will seek You and when I fall short, I will seek You all the more and repent and ask You to forgive and restore my relationship with You.

Day 44

1 John 3:13—Do not be surprised, my brothers and sisters, if the world hates you.

TRUTH:
"This person doesn't like me!" We start concerning ourselves with what others think of us at a very young age. Unfortunately, some people get so enamored with pleasing others that they will do almost anything to keep others in their life happy, even if that means being disobedient to God. However, God indicates that the world will hate us. Plus, their hatred of us shouldn't surprise us. The world that doesn't know Christ is not going to understand our motivation for doing what we do. But instead of worrying about them, we are to only be concerns about pleasing one person: God.

RESPONSE:
Father, it shouldn't surprise me when others question me or ridicule me for doing the things that please You. I will not be distracted by them and what they do. You are the only one I want to focus on and the only one I care about.

Day 45

1 John 3:14—We know that we have passed from death to life, because we love each other. Anyone who does not love remains in death.

TRUTH:
God is love. We learn love from the Father, and only because of his demonstration of love toward us though Jesus Christ are we able to experience and share true love. Love is a perfect measure of whether a person is truly following God. We cannot "work up" love and we can't manufacture love. Either we have God's love in our life that has saved us, or we do not and are still condemned to death. Is our life characterized by the love of God.

RESPONSE:
Father, You are love and because You live in me, You have saved me to love as You love. Show me how to love like You today in every situation I face. Only because of You and only through You am I able to live and show true love.

Day 46

1 John 3:15—Anyone who hates a brother or sister is a murderer, and you know that no murderer has eternal life residing in him.

TRUTH:
Our actions are born from our thoughts. What we are willing to consider in our thoughts, we would be willing to do in real life if the circumstance presented itself. When we think about hating people and the anger involved in that, Jesus Himself even stated that hatred is the same as murder. What thoughts do we allow in our minds? What thoughts do we dwell on? Our obedience to Christ begins with our thoughts, not just our actions.

RESPONSE:
Father, You are Holy and You see and know everything. You know my thoughts and I ask You to forgive me and cleanse me of any thoughts that don't glorify You. I must start with thoughts that honor and praise You so that my actions will do the same.

Day 47

1 John 3:16—This is how we know what love is: Jesus Christ laid down his life for us. And we ought to lay down our lives for our brothers and sisters.

TRUTH:

God is love and through Him we know what love is. He demonstrated love to us through the sacrifice of Jesus Christ on our behalf. Because we know what love is, we should act and respond the same to others. Our love for them is to be seen through our willingness to sacrifice ourselves for them. Do we show others that we love them or are we just saying the words? Does our love toward others look like Christ's love toward us?

RESPONSE:

Father, Your love is the standard and definition for what love truly is. You have displayed Your love to me in so many ways, but especially through the sacrifice of Jesus. Today, work through me to show others Your love. Allow my reactions and responses to demonstrate the sacrifice that is the true nature of love.

Day 48

1 John 3:17-18—If anyone has material possessions and sees a brother or sister in need but has no pity on them, how can the love of God be in that person? Dear children, let us not love with words or speech but with actions and in truth.

TRUTH:
We know that God is love and that He has commanded us to love. So what are we doing about it? Loving others is to be an action that we take, not just words or sentiments that we say. Loving others involves meeting their physical needs. We are to see others as Christ sees them and then treat them the way He would treat them. Are we demonstrating our love for other through actions and in truth?

RESPONSE:
Father, You are love, but You don't just tell me Your love; You show me love. I am to be the same way. Give me Your love for others that shares and encourages them and meets their needs.

Day 49

1 John 3:19-20—This is how we know that we belong to the truth and how we set our hearts at rest in his presence: If our hearts condemn us, we know that God is greater than our hearts, and he knows everything.

TRUTH:
God is truth, not our hearts. Our feelings can sway and change with time, but nothing changes the truth. God reminds us that if we've made a decision to follow Jesus, then we belong to the truth and nothing can change that. Some days we may not feel that way, but our feelings and emotions do not change what actually is the truth. Are we resting in the truth today?

RESPONSE:
Father, I will not believe my feelings; I will believe Your truth. I know that You are truth and through Jesus, I belong to the truth. This is true, no matter what I feel today. Keep my heart focused on You and Your truth today.

Day 50

1 John 3:21-22—Dear friends, if our hearts do not condemn us, we have confidence before God and receive from him anything we ask because we keep his commands and do what pleases him.

TRUTH:
Yesterday we talked about God's truth being greater than our own feelings. Today, when our feelings have come in line with the truth of God, we have such confidence in Him. We will receive anything from Him that we ask because we will be so in tune with Him that what we ask will be exactly in line with His will for us. Our actions will be pleasing to Him as we keep His commands. Are we in tune with God and are our hearts in line with His desires?

RESPONSE:
Father, I so greatly desire to have a close relationship with You. When I stumble and my heart doesn't always trust You completely, forgive me and help me see that You are my everything. I can place my total confidence in You and all that You have for me.

Day 51

1 John 3:23—And this is his command: to believe in the name of his Son, Jesus Christ, and to love one another as he commanded us.

TRUTH:
What does God command us to do? In the previous verse, it states that we keep his commands and do what pleases Him. Here, He tells us exactly what that is. We are to believe in the name of His Son Jesus Christ and we are to love each other. Are we following His commands? Would these two ideas describe our whole life? If not, we need to reevaluate and refocus today.

RESPONSE:
Father, You have told me exactly what I need to do in order to keep Your commands. Keep me focused on these two things today. I believe in Jesus Christ, Your Son, and I will concentrate on loving others, just as You command.

Day 52

1 John 3:24—The one who keeps God's commands lives in him, and he in them. And this is how we know that he lives in us: We know it by the Spirit he gave us.

TRUTH:
Yesterday, we saw that God's command for us is to believe in Jesus and love one another. Still, how do we know that God does what He promises us? God gives us His Spirit to live in us. Through the Holy Spirit, God lives in us and through us each day. We can have confidence in God and in all He has promised us because of His Spirit living in us.

RESPONSE:
Father, thank You for Your gift of the Holy Spirit. Thank You that we have confidence in You and Your promises. I know that through Your Holy Spirit living in me, I can know exactly what You have for me and I will trust in all that You do for me.

Day 53

1 John 4:1—Dear friends, do not believe every spirit, but test the spirits to see whether they are from God, because many false prophets have gone out into the world.

TRUTH:
How do we know whether an idea or a thought we've had comes from God? We can't just assume that all our thoughts are Godly because we have an enemy who would love to trip us up and cause us harm. Yet, God states that we can test the spirits to see whether they are from God or from our enemy. Anyone who comes and claims they are from God must be able to show and demonstrate that they are walking in truth. Tomorrow we will see exactly how to tell which is which, but as we go through today, we must be thinking about everyone and everything we encounter and be willing to go through and test each one.

RESPONSE:
Father, I must put my faith in You and no one else. You are the one who is truth and only those people who are walking with You will also be in truth. I will remain focused on You and only You today so that I may be able to test everything that comes my way as to whether or not it is from You.

Day 54

1 John 4:2—This is how you can recognize the Spirit of God: Every spirit that acknowledges that Jesus Christ has come in the flesh is from God.

TRUTH:
Jesus Christ is God and He came in the flesh to live among us and be the sacrifice to fulfill God's plan to provide for the salvation of those who believe. This is truth. The Spirit of God acknowledges that truth and professes that truth and always encourages actions that declare that truth. Anything else is from the evil one. These false spirits may try any and all sorts of deception, but when it comes down to it, only the Spirit of God will acknowledge and lead in God's truth. We can use this as a measure for everything that we are encouraged to do during the day. Does it meet this standard of truth?

RESPONSE:
Father, You will only ever encourage me to do things that are in line with Your truth. You have made a way for me and Your truth will always lead me. I will follow Your truth and will seek to test everything according to Your truth today. Keep my eyes open and my heart attuned to Your truth.

Day 55

1 John 4:3—but every spirit that does not acknowledge Jesus is not from God. This is the spirit of the antichrist, which you have heard is coming and even now is already in the world.

TRUTH:
Truly, the key to determining what is true or false, right or wrong, is found in Jesus Christ. No matter what people say or profess, we can always go back to their relationship and view of Jesus Christ. Do we use Christ as the measuring stick for every area in our life so that we may know and acknowledge the truth? Evil is in the world and we must be ready to discern between good and evil.

RESPONSE:
Father, I will keep my focus on Jesus Christ and will measure everything I encounter today next to Him to determine what is truth and what is not. Thank You for providing a way to see and to know what is true and what isn't so that I may follow You and not be deceived.

Day 56

1 John 4:4—You, dear children, are from God and have overcome them, because the one who is in you is greater than the one who is in the world.

TRUTH:
Remember all the evil and false spirits that were mentioned in the previous verses? The great news is that through God, we have overcome them all. God is greater than all the things that are of this world. As we surrender our lives to Him and allow Him to live in and through us, we see how great He is and we can trust Him to reign supreme over anything and everything we encounter today.

RESPONSE:
Father, You are over all, but sometimes I don't live like that is true. No matter the circumstance, no matter the situation or the temptation, You have overcome and through You, I will overcome, too. I will trust in You today and allow You to guide my every action and response so that Your power is evident through me.

Day 57

1 John 4:5—They are from the world and therefore speak from the viewpoint of the world, and the world listens to them.

TRUTH:
Still speaking about the false prophets, John reminds the people that the teachings and advice of the world will make sense to the world. People will listen to the false prophets and the false teachings. We must not be one of them who are deceived. Since we have Jesus living in us, we have overcome the false teaching and false teachers. However, we must not get distracted or discouraged when the world listens to them and their teachings. Remember, the world will listen to their own, but we have overcome the world.

RESPONSE:
Father, I praise You for overcoming the world. Sometimes it's very hard when the rest of the world seems to be following along with the things I know are wrong, but I will hold fast to You and Your teachings today. I will not be distracted when others seem to be going the wrong direction.

Day 58

1 John 4:6—We are from God, and whoever knows God listens to us; but whoever is not from God does not listen to us. This is how we recognize the Spirit of truth and the spirit of falsehood.

TRUTH:
When we start talking about doing the right thing in situations, we will have people who don't understand what we are saying or why we are saying it. They don't have the Spirit of God in them to help determine whether it is truth or falsehood. We shouldn't get upset or bothered by these people for they have been deceived by a spirit of falsehood. We should continue to pray for them so that they may come to a knowledge of God and receive His Spirit of truth.

RESPONSE:
Father, help me not get bothered when people don't understand Your truth. Help me to listen and speak only what Your Spirit of Truth gives me. I praise You and desire to be living in Your Truth, even if others don't understand.

Day 59

1 John 4:7-8—Dear friends, let us love one another, for love comes from God. Everyone who loves has been born of God and knows God. Whoever does not love does not know God, because God is love.

TRUTH:
God is love and because He is, we are able to be love to those we are around. We cannot truly love outside of God. People will try to love, but anything done outside of God is simply a cheap imitation and not true love. Do we know God and are we displaying God's love to everyone we come into contact with today? God is love.

RESPONSE:
Father, I will love as You love today. You have given me everything and only through You do I even know exactly what love is.

Day 60

1 John 4:9—This is how God showed his love among us: He sent his one and only Son into the world that we might live through him.

TRUTH:
God is love and because He is love, His actions all display His love. God sent Jesus Christ to come and live out the love of God for everyone to see. Jesus Christ's purpose for coming was so that we might be able to receive the love of God in our lives and be made right with God.

RESPONSE:
Father, You are love and through Jesus, You demonstrate Your love to me. I praise You and thank You for Your love and for how Your love can be lived out in my life daily.

Day 61

1 John 4:10—This is love: not that we loved God, but that he loved us and sent his Son as an atoning sacrifice for our sins.

TRUTH:
Without God sending Jesus to demonstrate love toward us, we would not know what love truly is. Because He sacrificed His Son, we are able to love others. God loved us even when we were at our most unloveable: buried in our sin and separated from God. Even then, God still showed us His love. Do we love others as God loves us?

RESPONSE:
Father, if I do not love others as You loved me, I'm not really showing love at all. You have given me everything and I will praise You for being the truest example of love. Thank You and I will honor You by showing the same love toward others.

Day 62

1 John 4:11—Dear friends, since God so loved us, we also ought to love one another.

TRUTH:
God showed us what love is because He Himself is love. Because we know what love is through Him, we are able to demonstrate that love to others. Not only are we able to do it, but we ought to do it since Christ lives in us and is able to love others through us. Will we let Christ love others through us today.

RESPONSE:
Father, You love me and have shown me that time and time again. Now use me today to show Your love to others so they may see You in everything that I do today.

Day 63

1 John 4:12—No one has ever seen God; but if we love one another, God lives in us and his love is made complete in us.

TRUTH:
We don't have to see God to know and feel His presence and His love in our lives. God is love and any time we love others or demonstrate love, we are displaying God for them to see. God's love is amazing and He allows us to live in His love each and every day.

RESPONSE:
Father, You are love and when You demonstrate love through me, You are showing the complete circle of who You are. I will live in Your love and will seek to help display that love to others.

Day 64

1 John 4:13-14—This is how we know that we live in him and he in us: He has given us of his Spirit. And we have seen and testify that the Father has sent his Son to be the Savior of the world.

TRUTH:
Two things testify of the relationship we have with Jesus: our words and our actions. First, God has given us His Spirit who lives in those who have believed in Him. Through the Spirit, we are able to act in such a way that displays our relationship with God. Second, the Spirit gives us the words to speak so that we are telling of our relationship with God to others. Does Christ live in us? If so, our words and actions should both demonstrate that.

RESPONSE:
Father, I praise You for giving me Your Spirit. I will speak and act today in a way that honors and displays You to everyone I am around. Thank You for Your Spirit that enables me to do that.

Day 65

1 John 4:15—If anyone acknowledges that Jesus is the Son of God, God lives in them and they in God.

TRUTH:

The message of salvation is simple to understand. If we will acknowledge that Jesus Christ is the perfect Son of God, admit that we have fallen short of God's expectations of us, and allow Jesus to take control of our life, then we will experience the joy of having God living in us. Do we have that close, personal relationship with God today?

RESPONSE:

Father, I know that Jesus Christ is God and I have asked Him to be the Lord of my life. I will live in You and You in me as I follow Your leading for my life.

Day 66

1 John 4:16—And so we know and rely on the love God has for us. God is love. Whoever lives in love lives in God, and God in them.

TRUTH:
Do we rely on God's love? God is love and He loves us, but it's not just a question of knowing God's love, but also relying on His love to lead us and guide us. Are we living each day relying on God's love?

RESPONSE:
Father, You are love and only by relying on You and Your love will I be able to live in love. I will choose to live in You today.

Day 67

1 John 4:17—This is how love is made complete among us so that we will have confidence on the day of judgment: In this world we are like Jesus.

TRUTH:
As it says in the previous verse, God is love and living in love means living in God and vice versa. This is how love is made complete. When we are living in God and allowing Him to live in us, we can have confidence that no matter what we face, we are exactly where God has us and doing His work. In that way, we are like Jesus, living in love each and every day. Has God and His love been made complete in us?

RESPONSE:
Father, You are love and through You, love is made complete in me. I will have confidence as I live in Your love, knowing that Your love also lives in me.

Day 68

1 John 4:18—There is no fear in love. But perfect love drives out fear, because fear has to do with punishment. The one who fears is not made perfect in love.

TRUTH:
Fear and love cannot co-exist. Either we are fully resting and trusting in God's love, or we are paralyzed by fear. Because of God's love and His promise to live in us and through us, we don't have to fear. Is there an area of our life where we are afraid? We can turn that over to God and choose to live in His love instead.

RESPONSE:
Father, when I am afraid, I will trust in You. Your love casts out all fear and I will rest in Your love knowing that I don't need to worry or fret, but trust in Your love.

Day 69

1 John 4:19—We love because he first loved us.

TRUTH:
This verse explains both the why and the how of love. Why do we love others? We love because he first loved us. How do we display love to others, even when they seem unloveable? God loves us first and through His living in us, He is able to love others through us. Because of God, we are both loveable and able to love.

RESPONSE:
Father, You loved me, even when I was in the midst of sin. You love me still. Every single day I am a part of Your wonderful love. I will praise You and lift You up. I will allow You to love others through me because You first loved me.

Day 70

1 John 4:20-21—Whoever claims to love God yet hates a brother or sister is a liar. For whoever does not love their brother and sister, whom they have seen, cannot love God, whom they have not seen. And he has given us this command: Anyone who loves God must also love their brother and sister.

TRUTH:
Our relationship with God is reflected in our relationship with others. If we are not loving toward our fellow believers, that is reflecting a bigger problem in our relationship with God. We can see and interact on a physical level with other believers and, as this verse says, we should be better able to love because of that since we haven't seen God physically. Are we loving others and treating others the same way that we love and treat God? If not, we are a liar.

RESPONSE:
Father, I will treat others as I treat You. I will love and respect them because I love and respect You. Give me Your love today as I go throughout my day.

Day 71

1 John 5:1—Everyone who believes that Jesus is the Christ is born of God, and everyone who loves the father, loves his child as well.

TRUTH:
We cannot separate our love of God and our love for Jesus. If we say we love God, we must also say we love His child as well. Jesus Christ is the Holy One of God, and He is God Himself. Loving and serving God means we must also love and serve Jesus. Do we see God and Jesus as One? Do we love both the same?

RESPONSE:
Father, You are love and You love me. I know that Your Son Jesus Christ is Holy, and I believe in Him and love Him as I love You. Help me explain that love and relationship to others today.

Day 72

1 John 5:2—This is how we know that we love the children of God: by loving God and carrying out his commands.

TRUTH:
John mentions it over and over again, but it all comes back to God and His love. Because of God, we are able to love others. The way we know we love others is because of our love for God. Out of love for Him, we are obedient to Him. By displaying love through obedience, we love God and others. All of this is possible because God Himself is love. Is God and His love central to everything in our life?

RESPONSE:
Father, You are love and through You, I am Your love. I will show Your love to others and to You through my obedience to You. Thank You for giving me Your love as You give me Yourself.

Day 73

1 John 5:3—In fact, this is love for God: to keep his commands. And his commands are not burdensome.

TRUTH:
What does it mean to love God? What does that look like? We show God that we love Him by obeying Him. Obedience is an act of love. God didn't make it so that showing our love for Him would be drudgery or would be viewed as a noose around our necks. Instead, God showed us that His commands come from His love and are easy to do when we are allowing Him to live and love through us. Are we joyfully showing God we love Him today?

RESPONSE:
Father, I will show You that I love You. Because of You, I am able to live in Your love and keep the commands that You have given. You command that I walk in love, so I will walk in You today as You live Your love through me.

Day 74

1 John 5:4-5—for everyone born of God overcomes the world. This is the victory that has overcome the world, even our faith. Who is it that overcomes the world? Only the one who believes that Jesus is the Son of God.

TRUTH:
We are overcomers through Jesus Christ. We have victory over the world and all that is in the world because we believe in and place our faith in the One who is victorious over the world. Are we living knowing that we have victory or are we living like we have been defeated? God has overcome the world and if we believe in Jesus and follow Him, we share in the victory!

RESPONSE:
Father, no matter how I feel or what I see when I look around, I will know that You have overcome the world and through You, I have overcome as well. I will not live today as if I am defeated, but instead I will remember that through Jesus, I am victorious.

Day 75

1 John 5:6—This is the one who came by water and blood—Jesus Christ. He did not come by water only, but by water and blood. And it is the Spirit who testifies, because the Spirit is the truth.

TRUTH:

Jesus Christ is God and man together. That was demonstrated throughout His entire ministry, but specifically at His baptism (water) and crucifixion (blood). At both of those events, the Spirit testified in remarkable ways that Jesus Christ is God in the flesh. Do we believe that Jesus Christ is fully and completely God while being fully man?

RESPONSE:

Father, I know that You sent Your Son Jesus to be fully man and fully God and that the Holy Spirit has testified to that truth over and over again through scripture. I pray that You will help me see more clearly today Your truth so that I may testify of the truth of who You are.

Day 76

1 John 5:7-8—For there are three that testify: the Spirit, the water and the blood; and the three are in agreement.

TRUTH:
In the Old Testament, the law required two or three witnesses when giving testimony in court. Here, John shares that the testimony of Jesus Christ is verified by three witnesses who are all in agreement. Do we know and understand the truth about Jesus Christ? We can share with confidence because we have such strong witnesses who are all in agreement that Jesus is fully God and fully man, just as He said He is.

RESPONSE:
Father, Your word is truth and all things testify to the truth of who You are and who Jesus Christ is. I will also testify today of that truth, knowing that You are who You say You are.

Day 77

1 John 5:9—We accept human testimony, but God's testimony is greater because it is the testimony of God, which he has given about his Son.

TRUTH:
God, through His Spirit, has testified as to who Jesus Christ is. In the previous verses, He explained that. But now, it is important to understand that since He is God, His testimony carries more weight and influence than any human's testimony about who they think Jesus is. Do we take God at His word or are we swayed and persuaded by men when thinking about Jesus Christ? We cannot believe in God and not believe what He says about His Son Jesus Christ.

RESPONSE:
Father, You have given us so much proof that Jesus Christ is the Messiah, the Holy One. I believe You and what You say, and I will follow Your testimony about Jesus. I will share with others who Jesus is, but ultimately, I will point them to You so that You can convince them of Jesus Christ.

Day 78

1 John 5:10—Whoever believes in the Son of God accepts this testimony. Whoever does not believe God has made him out to be a liar, because they have not believed the testimony God has given about his Son.

TRUTH:
Do we take God at His word? God has spoken and testified about His Son Jesus Christ. Do we believe His testimony? If we don't believe what God says about Jesus Christ, then we are calling God a liar. Do we believe Jesus Christ is the Son of God, fully man and fully God, who died to pay the penalty for our sins and redeem us into a relationship with God?

RESPONSE:
Father, I believe in Jesus Christ. I know and accept the truth of who He is based on who You say He is. I praise You for sending Him and today I will surrender even more completely to You.

Day 79

1 John 5:11-12—And this is the testimony: God has given us eternal life, and this life is in his Son. Whoever has the Son has the life; whoever does not have the Son of God does not have life.

TRUTH:

Here it is, the basics of the gospel message. God has given eternal life through His Son. If you have the Son, you have the life. If you don't, you don't. Everything boils down to the relationship with Jesus Christ. What do we believe and what will we do with Jesus Christ? God's gift of eternal life depends on our answer to that question.

RESPONSE:

Father, You are the giver of eternal life and that gift comes through Your Son, Jesus. You give life and I will trust in You. Only through my relationship with Jesus will I receive the eternal life that is promised.

Day 80

1 John 5:13—I write these things to you who believe in the name of the Son of God so that you may know that you have eternal life.

TRUTH:
In many other religions, the people simply wish they will have eternal life. They think they might. They try and try, but never really know for sure where they stand with their God. However, with the one true God, we can know. We can confidently, assuredly, know that we have eternal life. No wondering or doubting because God has written these things in His word to us so we can understand exactly how God provides eternal life for us who choose to follow and believe. Do we live today with the confident assurance of knowing we have eternal life?

RESPONSE:
Father, thank You for providing such assurance that I don't have to wonder or doubt my relationship with You. Through Your Son, You have given eternal life and I am confident that You will do as You say.

Day 81

1 John 5:14-15—This is the confidence we have in approaching God: that if we ask anything according to his will, he hears us. And if we know that he hears us—whatever we ask—we know that we have what we asked of him.

TRUTH:
When we pray, are we seeking God and His perfect will for our lives? We can be assured that He hears us. Even more than that, He gives us the assurance that He will provide what we ask according to His will. When we pray, are we praying for God's perfect will to be done? Do we seek after His will in every area of our lives? Then, once we have lifted up His will in prayer, do we have that blessed assurance that God will do what we have asked through His will?

RESPONSE:
Father, I will seek to pray for what is in Your will in each and every situation. I know that I can trust You to do all that You have promised. I will rest on You and Your promises knowing that since I have lifted Your will up to You in prayer, You will see it done.

Day 82

1 John 5:16—If you see any brother or sister commit a sin that does not lead to death, you should pray and God will give them life. I refer to those whose sin does not lead to death. There is a sin that leads to death. I am not saying that you should pray about that.

TRUTH:
While there is debate about what exactly is meant by a "sin that leads to death," we must realize that God desires that we lift one another up in prayer. Regardless of whether this refers to a sin that, when committed, results in the physical death of the sinner, or something along the lines of the unpardonable sin mentioned elsewhere in scripture, in either case, our support and prayers for our fellow believers is paramount. Do we lift each other up in prayer?

RESPONSE:
Father, You have placed other believers in my life and given me responsibility to pray for them. I lift up each one of them to You now. You know the areas where they struggle, and I pray You will give them Your strength to overcome today. Help them seek You and Your life in each decision they make today.

Day 83

1 John 5:17-18—All wrong doing is sin, and there is sin that does not lead to death. We know that anyone born of God does not continue to sin; the One who was born of God keeps them safe, and the evil one cannot harm them.

TRUTH:
When we accepted Jesus Christ as the Son of God, then we realize that He wants to live in and through us every day. He is the first One who was born of God when God raised Him from the dead. He leads and guides us to do those things that He would do. Will we lean on Him and allow Him to work through us? When we are following through with God, He will keep us safe from the evil one.

RESPONSE:
Father, I am not perfect, but You are. I will trust You and submit myself to You so that my deeds and thoughts will be totally in line with You and Your will. I trust You to lead me down the path that You have for me.

Day 84

1 John 5:19—We know that we are children of God, and that the whole world is under the control of the evil one.

TRUTH:
We are children of God, yet we are living in the enemy's camp. It can be very easy to get complacent and to let down our guard, but that is when we will be attacked. Our whole world is under Satan's control and if we do not guard ourselves, we will find ourselves falling into the trap of relying on the world and not on God. We are children of God. We must stay focused on our Father and on His desires.

RESPONSE:
Father, I praise You and lift You up for allowing me to be called Your child. I will never forget that my day to day life is lived in the camp of the enemy. Help me keep up my guard so I am not pulled down by the enemy.

Day 85

1 John 5:20-21—We know also that the Son of God has come and has given us understanding, so that we may know him who is true. And we are in him who is true by being in his Son Jesus Christ. He is the true God and eternal life. Dear children, keep yourselves from idols.

TRUTH:
God is the true God. Jesus Christ is the true redeemer. Anything else that we chase after is an idol. Do we keep ourselves from idols? Will we follow Him and trust Him to be who He says He is or will we not. Ultimately we are choosing Him or we are choosing idols. What will be our choice today?

RESPONSE:
Father, You are the One true God. You are the giver of life and only through You will I have true life. No idols for me, Father! Only You!

2 John

Day 86

2 John 1—The elder, to the lady chosen by God and to her children, whom I love in the truth— and not I only, but also all who know the truth—

TRUTH:
John begins his second letter to the churches reminding them of his love for them. Not just any love, but love in truth. Love that is not founded in the truth is not real love at all. The great part about true love is that it spreads. No only one person loves, but every person who knows the truth and is grounded in the truth has the same love. Are we sharing in the love of God that is grounded in His truth? That is the only way we can truly love one another.

RESPONSE:
Father, Your love is wonderful and amazing. You are truth and through Your truth I can know, experience, and share real love. Help me see Your truth clearer today so that I may love more like You.

Day 87

2 John 2—because of the truth, which lives in us and will be with us forever.

TRUTH:
The truth lives in us and will be with us forever. How is that possible? Jesus says in John 14:6 that He is the way, the truth, and the life. Jesus lives in us and will be with us forever. Do we live in the understanding that Jesus is the truth and that He lives in us and though us every day? We also can trust in His promise to be with us forever.

RESPONSE:
Father, You are the truth. You are the One who lives in us if we have accepted You. You will be with me forever, and I praise You for being with me throughout the day today!

Day 88

2 John 3—Grace, mercy, and peace from God the Father and from Jesus Christ, the Father's Son, will be with us in truth and love.

TRUTH:
Grace, mercy, and peace all sound so wonderful to have and experience. However, it's not just any grace, mercy, or peace; they must be completed together with truth and love. Only through the truth, Jesus Christ, and the love, God the Father, are we able to experience grace, mercy, and peace. Do we feel like we are lacking grace, mercy, and peace? We must seek after God the Father and the Father's Son so that we experience the truth and the love first, then we will see the grace, mercy, and peace.

RESPONSE:
Father, You are love and Jesus is the truth. Only through You will I experience grace, mercy, and peace. I surrender my life to You for only You bring about the grace, mercy, and peace that is needed in my life.

Day 89

2 John 4—It has given me great joy to find some of your children walking in the truth, just as the Father commanded us.

TRUTH:
We do not live the Christian life in a vacuum. We are surrounded by other believers and our obedience to God gives joy to them just as our disobedience brings grief to them. Similarly, their obedience and disobedience affects us. John received encouragement and joy knowing that the others were walking in the truth and following God's commands. Do we bring joy to other believers the same way? Do we rejoice in the obedience of fellow believers?

RESPONSE:
Father, You have given me such a family of brothers and sisters in You, and I love to hear of their faithfulness. I pray that I may also be a source of encouragement to others as I seek to walk today in Your truth.

Day 90

2 John 5—And now, dear lady, I am not writing you a new command but one we have had from the beginning. I ask that we love one another.

TRUTH:
John is not coming to the people with some new idea. He is writing to remind them of something they already know. They have been told and instructed in this from the beginning. John asks that they love one another. While this may seem to be an obvious statement, it stands to reason that since he mentioned it, they had not been doing it. Do we focus on loving one another? Do we need to be reminded of the importance of loving one another? We must be careful that even though it is a simple statement, that we don't overlook it or place less importance on it because it is truly the foundation of understanding who God is.

RESPONSE:
Father, it's easy to get distracted. You have commanded that I love one another, yet sometimes circumstances come up and take my focus away from You and Your command to love. Forgive me and place my focus firmly back on what You desire; that I love one another.

Day 91

2 John 6—And this is love: that we walk in obedience to his commands. As you have heard from the beginning, his command is that you walk in love.

TRUTH:
Looking for a definition of love? Here is one: love is walking in obedience to God's commands. It is impossible to consider something love if it does not come from the commands of God. God is love and only as we seek to imitate Him will we be able to move and work as He desires. That is how we will display God's love through us. Also, loving is not just a request, but a command. We are to walk in love, which is obedience to His commands.

RESPONSE:
Father, I love You and as a result, I desire to follow Your commands. Help me to see and obey Your commands so that I may easily follow. I choose to walk in love today.

Day 92

2 John 7—I say this because many deceivers, who do not acknowledge Jesus Christ as coming in the flesh, have gone out into the world. Any such person is the deceiver and the antichrist.

TRUTH:
We must be on our guard. There are many deceivers who are out in the world, not just one or two. These people don't acknowledge Jesus Christ. These people try to distract us from carrying out His command to walk in love. We will face opposition and distraction to God's commands in our life. How will we respond?

RESPONSE:
Father, keep me on the lookout for the deceivers who try to distract me from following Your command to love. I will keep my eyes focused on You so that I am not tricked or deceived into focusing on someone or something else.

Day 93

2 John 8—Watch out that you do not lose what we have worked for, but that you may be rewarded fully.

TRUTH:
Those deceivers mentioned in the previous verse are hard at work and if we are not careful and watching, we will lose focus and get distracted. God has a plan and a purpose for us and we must be careful that we are focused on Him and His plan or else we will miss out on all the rewards and blessings that He has in store for us. Do we want to be fully rewarded in all that God has planned and purposed for our life? We must watch out and be on our guard.

RESPONSE:
Father, I will stay focused on You and watch out for others seeking to lead me astray. I want all that You want for me, including a full reward. Keep me focused and alert every minute of every day.

Day 94

2 John 9—Anyone who runs ahead and does not continue in the teaching of Christ does not have God; whoever continues in the teaching has both the Father and the Son.

TRUTH:
We love to run ahead. Even as little children we race ahead of our parents and have to be reminded to come back. So often, we do the same with God. We don't want to wait or go His pace, so we race ahead, trying to find our way on our own. When we do that, we are not following Christ's teachings or obeying God. We must learn to wait on Him and walk with Him, not race ahead.

RESPONSE:
Father, You know where to go and You know the best pace to get there. I will walk with You and not try to run ahead of You. I will follow Your teachings and seek to obey You.

Day 95

2 John 10—If anyone comes to you and does not bring this teaching, do not take them into your house or welcome them.

TRUTH:
False teaching is a serious issue. There are plenty of people who teach false ideas about God: who He is, what He is like, how to be made right with Him. The popular definition of "tolerance," where we are to just allow people to believe whatever they want, is wrong. We have the truth and God desires that we hold to His truth. Do we stand up for God's truth?

RESPONSE:
Father, I will not believe the lie that it is okay to believe whatever I want. I will hold to Your truth and seek to share that truth in love. You are worthy of my devotion, and I will not be led astray by false teaching or allow those teachers to continue unchallenged. I will hold to and protect Your truth.

Day 96

2 John 11—Anyone who welcomes them shares in their wicked work.

TRUTH:
We don't have to actively participate in sin to be guilty of sharing in it. According to this verse, even if we just sit back and do nothing, we are essentially welcoming it in and are therefore guilty. We must be actively standing up against the evil and false teachings that are so prevalent in the world today. If we are not actively standing up to kick that garbage out, then we are guilty of welcoming it in.

RESPONSE:
Father, help me not to be passive about the false teachings that are around. Give me courage and boldness to stand up against them. I will not sit by and passively allow sin to prosper and spread.

Day 97

2 John 12—I have much to write to you, but I do not want to use paper and ink. Instead, I hope to visit you and talk with you face to face, so that our joy may be complete.

TRUTH:
God did not design the Christian life to be lived in a vacuum. He desires that we share with others face to face. We are so encouraged to see each other face to face and share in the message and encouragement of God. John knew that and desired to be together with the other believers as much to encourage himself as to encourage them. Do we look forward to meeting together with other believers? Only as we come together we can experience that joy.

RESPONSE:
Father, thank You for friends who believe in You and with whom I can share and encourage and find joy together. I will seek out other believers and will not try to live this Christian life on my own.

Day 98

2 John 13—The children of your sister, who is chosen by God, send their greetings.

TRUTH:
Their sister, another church, also sends greetings. The churches were designed to work together to encourage one another and to stand with each other as together we stand for God's truth. Churches are not meant to compete against one another for members, or argue and fuss with one another. Do we partner with other Bible-believing churches? Are we working together with other churches that also seek to follow God? We can accomplish so much more as we follow God together than we can on our own.

RESPONSE:
Father, thank You, not just for other believers, but for other believing churches that I can work together with to accomplish Your will for Your glory. I will seek out those who believe in You and follow Your truths and will work together.

3 John

Day 99

3 John 1—The elder, to my dear friend Gaius, whom I love in truth.

TRUTH:
John, writing here, gives a great definition of friendship. Gaius was a dear friend that John loved in truth. Friendship should always be based on truth and not lies, however, even more special is when the friendship is based on "The Truth," Jesus Christ. Do we define our relationship with others by our relationship with Christ? We should use that definition and allow our relationship with Jesus Christ to impact everyone else in our life.

RESPONSE:
Father, I love You and I love that You are truth. Please keep me focused on You first today so that every other relationship I have will be defined by my relationship with You.

Day 100

3 John 2 — Dear friend, I pray that you may enjoy good health and that all may go well with you, even as your soul is getting along well.

TRUTH:
Our spiritual health and our physical health are both important and need to be addressed in our lives. Are we taking care of ourselves physically? What about spiritually? If we are neglecting our spiritual life, then we will not know or be ready for the plans that God has for us. If we are neglecting our physical health, then we may know God's plans for us, but not be able to do everything that God would like to use us for in His work. We must pray for and devote time to improving both.

RESPONSE:
Father, it's easy to think that You only care about our spiritual life and health, but you care about all of me. Help me to focus on my physical health as well, and be sure that as I am able to focus on You spiritually, I am also ready physically to do the things You ask of me.

Day 101

3 John 3—It gave me great joy when some believers came and testified about your faithfulness to the truth, telling how you continue to walk in it.

TRUTH:
What would another believer say about you if they were giving a report to this verse's author, John? Would John be encouraged and joyful, or disappointed and embarrassed? Others are always watching and the way we live our lives is a testimony of what we believe. Do we daily walk in the path that would bring joy to another believer? Are we faithful to God's truth each day through the seemingly mundane activities of life or are we lazy in our faith? People are watching and waiting to testify about what they see in our lives. What will they say?

RESPONSE:
Father, I desire that You have joy when You think of me. Give me the strength and courage to live today faithfully and consistently following Your word. You are my desire, so help me to live that out to bring joy to other believers.

Day 102

3 John 4—I have no greater joy than to hear that my children are walking in the truth.

TRUTH:
It is unknown whether John had any biological children, yet he had scores of spiritual children. The people that he led to Christ and discipled to grow in Christ were all his children. Just like with parents and biological children, other people would come up to John and say, "I saw this child of yours doing this." When John had great reports about his children, he felt pride and joy in knowing they were pleasing God. Do we have spiritual children? If not, why not? If we do, are we influencing and encouraging them to continue in the right path?

RESPONSE:
Father, thank You for the spiritual children you have brought into my life. I pray You will continue to guide me and bring me to parent even more spiritual children. Keep me focused on You so that my spiritual children may be focused on You as well.

Day 103

3 John 5—Dear friend, you are faithful in what you are doing for the brothers and sisters, even though they are strangers to you.

TRUTH:
No matter where we are or what we are doing, we have a relationship with other Christians in the world. We are to pray for them and support them and lift them up even if we don't know them personally. When they hurt, we hurt for we are all part of the body of Christ. Do we look for ways to be faithful and show our support for our brothers and sisters in Christ around the world?

RESPONSE:
Father, I am part of Your wonderful family and have so many brothers and sisters in Christ! Please keep me mindful of them so that I can be faithful to them and pray for them and support them in any way You lead. I don't have to know their names or have met them personally in order to love and support them for they are Your children, too. You love them, so I love them.

Day 104

3 John 6—They have told the church about your love. Please send them on their way in a manner that honors God.

TRUTH:
Do we show excellent hospitality skills? In the culture when this was written, hospitality was extremely important, but here John gives a new definition of true hospitality: "send them on their way in a manner that honors God." When we meet people, when we work with people, or anytime we interact with people, are we sending them on their way in a manner that honors God?

RESPONSE:
Father, keep me focused on this today so that every person I encounter today will feel like they have encountered the living God. Help me be compassionate and always seeking to honor You in every interaction today.

Day 105

3 John 7—It was for the sake of the Name that they went out, receiving no help from the pagans.

TRUTH:
When we are going about the work that God has provided for us to do, those who don't believe in God will not understand and not be of help. We shouldn't expect them to be. When we are following God, we should expect to receive help from God. Others who believe in God and are following God will also be able to help us, but unless the person has that understanding of why we are going about doing the work of God in the first place, they will not truly be able to help us or direct us and may, in fact, get in our way. Who are we asking for help as we seek to do the work God has for us to do?

RESPONSE:
Father, I will follow You and do all that You desire, knowing that the strength and help to do those things comes from You. I will not look for spiritual help from others who don't know You because they don't understand why I am doing Your work. You are the One I will follow and from You, I will receive help.

Day 106

3 John 8—We ought therefore to show hospitality to such people so that we may work together for the truth.

TRUTH:
"Show hospitality," "work together," and "for the truth" are all phrases that really stand out in this verse. Do we actually act out and demonstrate the kindness of hospitality? Do we foster and encourage Christians to work together, and when we work together, is it for the purpose of sharing the truth of Jesus Christ? These are great questions that we can ask about everything that we do. As we examine our life today, what are the answers?

RESPONSE:
Father, give me a spirit of hospitality to demonstrate Your love to others. I desire to work together with other believers in order to share Your truth. Please bring me together with the people You desire to be able to do that today.

Day 107

3 John 9—I wrote to the church, but Diotrophes, who loves to be first, will not welcome us.

TRUTH:
It's hard to imagine a church leader like John not being welcome in the church, yet that is exactly what he writes here. Instead, a prideful and arrogant man refused to welcome him. You see, when someone loves to be first, they will turn away anyone who might threaten their number 1 position. Do we think more highly of ourselves than we should? That pride can blind us to people and circumstances around us. Do we love to be first? If so, we will always turn away others who might be able to help and encourage us along the way.

RESPONSE:
Father, I don't want to be first. I want You to be first in my life. I want to be open to all that You have for me and if I place myself first, then I will miss out on Your best for me. I welcome You to come and work and move in my life in whatever way You see fit.

Day 108

3 John 10—So when I come, I will call attention to what he is doing, spreading malicious nonsense about us. Not satisfied with that, he even refuses to welcome other believers. He also stops those who want to do so and puts them out of the church.

TRUTH:
John goes into more detail about the situation he brought up in the previous verse. Diotrophes is spreading lies, refusing hospitality, and then throwing out of the church those who are being hospitable. What is John going to do? He plans to confront Diotrophes and call out what he is doing wrong. There are sins and evil in the world that make God angry. We must stand up for what is right and confront evil through Christ. Are we willing to follow God's leading to stand up against the wrongs we see?

RESPONSE:
Father, it's so much easier to just complain about the evil in this world than it is to stand up against it. Give me courage, boldness and a love for You that will not let me keep silent about the evil and injustice in this world. You are against it, and so am I!

Day 109

3 John 11—Dear friend, do not imitate what is evil but what is good. Anyone who does what is good is from God. Anyone who does what is evil has not seen God.

TRUTH:
Sometimes we try to make things so complicated, yet following Christ is really this easy. We are to imitate what is good and through Him working and moving in our lives, we will do what is good and what is of God. Who or what are we trying to be like today? God is to be our example for how to respond in every situation.

RESPONSE:
Father, You are good and everything good comes from You. I want to be an imitator of all that You think and do. Lead me and my actions today.

Day 110

3 John 12—Demetrius is well spoken of by everyone—and even by the truth itself. We also speak well of him, and you know that our testimony is true.

TRUTH:
A lot of people are speaking well of Demetrius, but the most important thing is that the truth speaks well of him. Demetrius is lining up with the truth. It doesn't matter who speaks well of us, if we are not following the truth and having the truth speak well of us, we have missed it. As the old saying goes: please God, and those who please God will be pleased with you. All you can do is pray for the rest.

RESPONSE:
Father, following Your truth is my focus today. I desire to be more like You and to live out Your truth. I will not get disturbed by what others are thinking. You have provided everything I need and my focus is on pleasing You.

Day 111

3 John 13—I have much to write to you, but I do not want to do so with pen and ink.

TRUTH:
In today's world it is so easy to send an email or text and think that takes care of everything. We use written words to communicate a lot of things. However, even back in this day and time, John recognized the need for personal connection. How much time do we spend face to face or voice to voice with others? We can create such strong connections with people if we will take the time to actually call or meet with others. Do we show people we value them by being willing to meet with them or are we only spending impersonal emails? God wants to meet personally with us. Take the time today to share God's love and encouragement with someone in person.

RESPONSE:
Father, I have become so reliant on impersonal means of communication with others, but You are a very personal God who desires deep connection with people. I pray you will give me the opportunity to connect with someone today beyond just an email or text. I know You desire personal connection and so do I.

Day 112

3 John 14—I hope to see you soon, and we will talk face to face. Peace to you. The friends here send their greetings. Greet the friends there by name.

TRUTH:
Personal connection and the peace of God: they go together. We have a great opportunity to experience and share that peace with others every single day. When we connect with others, do we convey the peace and assurance that God has everything worked out? We can work together to strengthen each other and to experience God's perfect peace.

RESPONSE:
Father, I am stronger together with other believers than I am apart. Your peace is more easily felt when I share it with other believers. I will seek Your encouragement today, for often that encouragement is found in and through other believers.

About the Author

Several years ago, God led Kristi Burchfiel through some difficult times in her personal life. Only by studying and applying the truths found in the Bible did she find the answers she needed to get her life back on track.

Now, Kristi works daily to continue putting those truths into practice. She is passionate about studying and applying the Bible and invites others to share in the peace and direction of God found through the truths in God's word.

Kristi, her husband D, and their two children currently make their home in Wichita, Kansas.

Website – www.kristiburchfiel.com
Twitter –
http://twitter.com/#!/kristiburchfiel
Facebook -
http://www.facebook.com/#!/pages/Without-Regrets-A-Study-of-Ecclesiastes/122149427808582

Also by Kristi Burchfiel

Bible Studies:

The Decay Within: A Study of Amos

Amazon:
http://amzn.com/1618620142

Tate Publishing:
http://www.tatepublishing.com/bookstore/book.php?w=978-1-61862-014-9

Without Regrets: A Study of Ecclesiastes

Amazon:
http://amzn.com/1615665005

Tate Publishing:
http://www.tatepublishing.com/bookstore/book.php?w=978-1-61566-500-6

Coming early 2015—Piecing Together Forgiveness: A Study of Philemon

The Daily Devotional Series:

The Daily Devotional Series: Gospel of John
The Daily Devotional Series: Genesis
The Daily Devotional Series: Psalm volume 1
The Daily Devotional Series: Psalm volume 2
The Daily Devotional Series: Psalm volume 3
The Daily Devotional Series: 365 Devotions Through the New Testament
The Daily Devotional Series: 1 & 2 Chronicles
The Daily Devotional Series: Proverbs

How to Become a Christian

- We are all sinners
  - Romans 3:23—*for all have sinned and fall short of the glory of God*
- The result of our sin is that we all deserve death
  - Romans 6:23—*For the wages of sin is death, but the free gift of God is eternal life in Christ Jesus our Lord.*
- God paid the penalty for our sins on our behalf through the death of his Son, Jesus Christ
  - Romans 5:8—*But God demonstrates His own love toward us, in that while we were yet sinners, Christ died for us.*
- When we acknowledge our sin and understand God's free gift of salvation, accept God's gift and allow Him to be Lord of our life, he saves us.
  - Romans 10:9-10, 13—*that if you confess with your mouth Jesus as Lord, and believe in your heart that God raised Him from the dead, you will be saved; for with the heart a person believes, resulting in righteousness, and with the mouth he confesses, resulting in salvation. For whoever will call on the name of the Lord will be saved.*

Admit that you are a sinner, believe that God has provided a way through Jesus for you to be saved, and confess or pray to God and ask Him to be the Lord of your life. He loves you!

John 1:12—*But as many as received Him, to them He gave the right to become the children of God, even to those who believe in His name.*

Made in the USA
San Bernardino, CA
16 January 2020